Pen in the
Spirit
⊕ One More Time

MICHAEL P. MALLARDI

ARPress
ILLUMINATING IDEAS
EMPOWERING VOICES

ARPress
45 Dan Road Suite 5
Canton MA 02021

Hotline: 1(888) 821-0229
Fax: 1(508) 545-7580

Ordering Information:

Quantity sales. Special discounts are available on quantity purchases by corporations, associations, and others. For details, contact the publisher at the address above.

Printed in the United States of America.

ISBN-13:   Softcover   979-8-89676-017-7
              eBook   979-8-89676-018-4

Library of Congress Control Number: 2024925452

Table of Contents

FOREWARD

One day in August 1987, I decided to take a break from the office and go for a walk. I strolled up the Avenue of the Americas in New York City, intending either to go to a bookstore on Fifth Avenue (to my right) or Central Park (to my left); when I had an unusual experience. I heard a male voice distinctly telling me to go to the Lady Chapel. The Lady Chapel is in the apse of St. Patrick's Cathedral. And I did so.

After settling in a chapel pew, I noticed a gray booklet beside me. It was face down with the invitation: Free Pamphlet - Please Take. Little did I realize how profoundly my life would be affected by a booklet. It was entitled, "Our Lady of Medjugorje." Medjugorje is a small village in Bosnia-Hercegovina where the Virgin Mary has been said to appear.

After reading the booklet, I took stock of myself and then vowed to practice my faith seriously, devoting myself especially to daily mass and the rosary. Subsequently, I visited Medjugorje twice and was party to several occurrences that validated my earlier commitment.

Several months after my first visit, I came across a passage from the prophet Isaiah (30:21) who wrote 2,700 years ago: "From behind a voice shall sound in your ears. This is the way walk in it. Whether you would turn to the right or the left." I'm following that way and it's been an interesting and rewarding journey. I encourage you to do the same.

To the Reader

No poet was I and my inkwell dry,
Until inspired by the Spirit's grace.
Now from 'Desert' to 'Love,'
And prompts from above,
I even explore the mystery of space.

Time and again He moves me to pen,
About God and His relation to men.
Visiting places long out of mind,
On a journey with joy at its end.

~~~~~~~

Pen in the Spirit – One More Time is the
third book in The Pen in the Spirit series.
Characterized as a love story by a
reader of the first book; a homilist
subsequently opined the ones who come to
know God best are mystics and poets.

I hope you will find both still to be true.

WHAT IS LOVE?

Love is more than a feeling,
The beat of a tremulous heart.
An ephemeral taste at the table,
A touch of a cheek as we part.

The kiss in the dark we desire,
A strand brushed away from one's eyes.
Caresses remembered forever,
An embrace we decry 'cause we're shy.

A polka-dot dress on a maiden,
Her smile when she bids us goodbye.
Like people we cherished forever,
A life we miss so we cry.

Nature, too, is a beloved,
Like a mountain that pierces the sky.
A bird taught to fly by its mother,
Streams aflow that never run dry.

A beloved presumes a lover,
Someone with something to share.
A devotion to rise to the occasion,
For a maiden that's lovely 'n' fair.

Manifestations, all, of life's essence,
A benison from The Creator on high.
Whose Spirit animates our choices,
True love that will never say die.

February 2024

STORIES

I feel your presence in the darkness,
To protect myself from me.
Ever attentive to my struggles,
You listen to my pleas.

You strengthen me in weakness,
Sufficient to my needs.
Who knows me from forever,
And knows of all my deeds.

Despite my imperfections,
My cup you fill and bless.
Yet I know you expect more from me,
Than those you've given less.

On those occasions, prod me,
When the dark one tempts my soul.
Seduces me with outre tales,
'til imagination takes its toll.

It's only You, The Word, I need,
Who's more valuable than gold.
Gave Your all to make us whole,
The Greatest Story Ever Told.

October 2024

WHERE'S HEAVEN?

It must be far above me,
I know it's in the sky.
The kingdom I aspire to,
When it's time for me to die.

Could be lightyears from Andromeda,
A bit beyond the stars.
Where Libra strums a ten-string lyre,
With melodies from Mars.

I'm told it's where angels sing,
Before a golden throne.
Whose gates of pearl have opened wide,
For those who have atoned.

Where the Holy Face will smile at us,
If our admittance is for real.
Where only His wounds may sparkle,
For ours He would have healed.

Where purity reigns 'n' there is no pain,
For eternity of bliss.
Where joy enfolds for untold years,
And nothing is amiss.

It's a place of pure happiness,
No matter where it lies.
And it comes with a guarantee,
There is no better prize.

November 2024

THE SHEPHERD

In the shadows of the evening,
There appeared a glimpse of light.
A flicker of a firefly,
To guide me through the night.

A pilgrim on life's journey,
Walking staff in hand.
Trying to access higher realms,
And sheep grazing on the land.

There to find the Holy Shepherd,
High among the rocks.
Cradling an unblemished lamb,
In retribution for the flock.

Forever on the out-look,
For the one that lost its way.
Found at last, before it passed,
To forage one more day.

I pray someday he'll caress me,
When my fleece turns lily white.
Carry me home on his shoulders,
When it's time to say goodnight.

November 2024

CHOICES

"An apple a day will keep the doctor away,
Said a misguided Eve to Adam.
For heaven's sake, it was only a snake,
Seemed more upset with the leaves 'round my bottom."

Choices, choices, a multitude of choices,
Some of greater import than others.
Some one-to-one, others undone,
In conflict with sisters and brothers.

Causes of war, are the options ignored,
When wisdom isn't asked to the table.
For many are swayed by choices not made,
Rebuilding the Tower of Babel.

When our time has come and we're one 'n' done,
It's God's choice to make and His only.
But each has been assigned an appropriate place,
To expire yet never be lonely.

The right of choice is most often voiced,
Repeatedly throughout creation.
Over 'n' over some choose as they oughta,
Only to face fear and rejection.

The right to choose and the outcomes pursued,
Depend upon a principled and moral society.
Otherwise, a single choice can make matters worse,
Without any sense of propriety.

November 2024

OUR LADY OF THE ROSARY

She stands there in effigy,
But sees after me each night.
Guards me and protects me,
After turning out the light.

Fifty legions of her angels,
Nine tribunes in command.
The Prince of Peace as vanguard,
Heaven's weapon in her hand.

She's there because I need her,
But she requires, too, I fight.
For demons are persistent,
Deeming night is theirs by right.

Just a rosary said in silence,
May be enough to quell our fears.
For we sense our Blessed Mother,
Who'll wipe away our tears.

If the battle is ongoing,
Stay the course and don't despair.
'cause with the weapon of the ages,
They'll retreat to Satan's lair.

Our Lady of the Rosary,
Modestly clad in blue and white.
Made the difference at Lepanto,*
And can do so every night.

October 2024

*Where outnumbered Christians defeated a superior, Ottoman-Turk Armada in 1571.
The defeat attributed to the recitation of The Rosary throughout Christendom
requested by Pope Pius V.

GLORY BE!

We raise our praise to Thee each day,
O Triune God above.
The Holy Three adored as one,
The Living God of Love.

Hear our plea that we might enjoy,
Paradise anon with Thee.
Where the Tree of Knowledge 'n' the Tree of Life,
Now rejoice with a leafless tree.

A tree so rare, all may share,
In the ransom paid to Thee.
Stained with blood, shed in love,
In fealty by the Son of Three.

Forever green will forever mean,
An eternal life with Thee.
Arrayed in light 'ere the holiest of sights,
Aside a crystal and merciful sea.

O glorious Lord, 'slain by the sword,'
So all might be saved and free.
Please make whole, Your chosen souls,
So we might sing Halleluiah 'n' Glory Be!

October 2024

CANTICLE OF MT. TABOR

I long to see your face, O Lord,
Disfigured on the way to your tree.
Whose glory has long been recovered,
So humanity could be rescued 'n' free.

His glorified body on Mount Tabor,
Appeared to the holiest of eyes.
When Elijah and Moses met The Christ,
And three apostles, in witness, aside.

Pleased by the Father was He the Son,
Willingly prepared to die.
An unblemished lamb within the halls of IAM,
Where it's sacrifice fell short of His Rise.

He alerted them both Heaven 'n' Earth,
Now that His time had arrived.
For Him, to suffer, die, and rise once again,
Thus having a chance to survive.

He awaits for us now, wounds aflow 'n' afire,
In accordance with God's design.
That they may be seen, over the widest ravine,
Just as the stars in the firmament shine.

O Mystical Body, O Glorified Lord,
Transfigured and Glory Be.
We want to ascend 'n' hope to attend,
The majesty and Godhead of Three.

November 2024

THE SKY

How lovely the sky,
When the sun starts to rise.
Sheds its gray coat,
As the colors arrive.

Becomes bluer than blue,
'less the clouds bid it hide.
But will eventually peek through,
To brighten outside.

Lofty and true with an invisible hue,
To enable our vision 'n' enhance our view.
It's unseen though ethereal,
So we can still see it's blue.

It carries the clouds,
And enables birds fly.
When burdened with water,
It lets the clouds cry.

Tho' it's there through the day,
It seems gone through the night.
But it is just beyond the moon beams,
And will return when it's light.

November 2024

STORMY WEATHER

The dividing line 'twixt dark 'n' shine,
Presages what's our due.
For stormy clouds overhead,
Quickly pass on through.

Gusts ahead of a darkened sky,
As it blows in from the East.
See clouds rail high and tumble nigh,
As we feel the wind increase.

Slanting rain besiege the panes,
To wash the glass anew,
See a race of raindrops fall,
To dramatize the view.

The storm ebbs when the sun peeks through,
And raindrops wane away.
But there's still time for love today,
Let me count the ways.

November 2024

FORGIVENESS AT SEA

Consoling graces scour the traces,
Of the unending bed of the sea.
Ready to pour a balm of salvation,
On the wounds from a distended tree.

No matter how dark, regardless how deep,
Despite how often the need.
The currents flow to resolve every woe,
Disclosed fully on recalcitrant knees.

Every sin that we rue, confessed when they're due,
May be fully pardoned at sea.
But sins not explained, may be fully retained,
If scarlet appears on the kelp that we see.

Repeatedly wrong, we sing the same song,
Again, forgive me, it's once more for me.
For try as I may, goodness eludes me each day,
And I must reapply for a bath in the sea.

November 2024

CHRISTMAS MOON

The Christmas Moon before the yule,
Rose on a star-lit night.
Witnessed a birth in a make-shift site,
Shadowed by the Spirit 'n' divine of right.

Illuminated a cave for Him who saves,
A two-natured Trinitarian child.
Held at the breast of a mother at rest,
Forever immaculate and mild.

Came in the flesh at the Father's behest,
In payment of an unpaid debt.
Broadcast God's news, so we be renewed,
By a sacrifice that overcame death.

Now we celebrate His life, when the moon's just right,
With evergreens trimmed in lights.
Tinsel and balls, gingerbread for all,
Candle-lit windows at night.

Gifts, too, are exchanged 'neath the tree they surround,
In memory of God's largesse.
And carols are sung 'n' silver bells rung,
To express the joy professed.

Tho' the gift of Himself, is the very best gift,
That appeased our original fall.
He comes as a host of unleavened bread,
For the benefit and redemption of all.

November 2024

WAR AND PEACE

Bodies, bodies everywhere,
Too many to ignore.
Corpses, corpses victimized,
The consequence of war.

Pride and greed the genesis,
Of cordite in the air.
The innocent and gullible,
Who share in war's despair.

Innocence on a bicycle,
Old women in a store.
Dog tags and body bags,
All casualties of war.

Marching bands to loud applause,
With promises of more.
Pomp and circumstance to preen the soul,
'spite the aftermath in store.

Evil often rears its head,
And deserves to be deplored.
Must be resisted with all our might,
But be sure there's nothing more.

Don't be quick to join the mob,
Just to be of one accord.
Remember God loves all of us,
And the pen is mightier than the sword.

September 2024

THE LASS

Just a lass, when it came to pass,
She was hailed as full of grace.
"Blessed art thou among women," he said,
And The Pride of the human race.

Her resounding "yes" to the angel's request,
Caused heaven and Earth to rejoice.
For from her would come, God's only son,
The Word and God's human voice.

Before kine and shepherds in a stable at night,
A child in her arms came to light.
A water-trough with straw, was the creche they saw,
While His throne remained out of sight.

From swaddling clothes to the red robe He wore,
The crown of spines that He bore.
The suffering servant who suffered death,
Would return to His throne once more.

Later in life, she recalled the strife,
Forewarned at her child's presentation.
When a sword pierced her heart, to reveal many thoughts,
And her sorrowful role in salvation.

Now stars can be seen, round the head of the Queen,
Who went further than any other.
For she forever reigns in the Trinity's name,
As the Immaculate Lass and Mother.

September 2024

DEEPER STILL

Do we fully appreciate how He suffered,
The depth of His travail.
Beyond the scourge and hammers,
Besides the cross and nails.

The God-man's thirst and hunger,
His disappointment at our fails.
The vermin and filth encountered,
The night before in jail.

The loss of far too many,
In the future He foresaw.
The opprobrium and rejection,
By those He fed in scores.

The burden of our ransom,
On a leafless tree twice sawn.
After all He had created,
Stained until reborn.

Rued the tears of a sorrowful mother,
Who in time a queen becomes.
Held at her breast as an infant,
And a lifeless lamb and Son.

He rose again in glory,
And death was overcome.
But disbelief 'n' sacrilege continue,
To the detriment of some.

Look beyond the figure crucified,
Consider the horrors He endured.
That reluctant hearts be opened,
And salvation be assured.

September 2024

DESERTS

When birds of a feather,
Flew without feathers,
And forests were replete with fear.
Roars could be heard to unnerve the bravest,
Since the prospect was harsh 'n' severe.

Water flowed aplenty to slake the land,
And dense was the mist 'til it rose.
The sky was red, bespeaking of dread,
And its botany lush in appose.

Fearsome beasts ravaged at will,
Even terrorizing the large with their might.
Then amphibians appeared evolving in time,
Soon feathered 'n' taking to flight.

Now, the sand blows,
Where the events we suppose.
Occurred o'er the eons of night.
For deserts now reign, with the absence of rain,
Bathed in the sun's torrid light.

September 2024

PENNIES

Copper pennies in my pocket,
Hear the jingles – feel the change.
'tween the nickels 'n' the quarters,
Lie the thin ones just the same.

Penny-wise and often foolish,
I confess to my excess.
Only coins are in my pocket,
'cause I squandered all the rest.

A penny saved earns a penny,
But not enough to pay my debts.
So I took a chance or two,
And lost to my regret.

Only want what you need, they say,
It's solvency's safest bet.
A word to the tempted,
Lest in weakness they forget.

September 2024

ODE TO A WATERMELON

Round 'n' green with a modest sheen,
A picnic basket's treat.
Rhizome–bred head-to-head,
A watery delight to eat.

Halved or quartered to suit the host,
Sliced red and white and green.
Succulent as well in chunks 'n' cubes,
A melon lover's dream.

A sweet delight when grown just right,
An oasis within a rind.
Rosy-red, sparsely seeded,
The kind we hope to find.

The kind of fruit, to tell the truth,
I wish I could enjoy all year.
Only to hear they can be grown indoors,
And that's all one had to hear.

So I sit inside 'n' swallow my pride,
And munch the whole day long.
Tho, often not red, but pale instead,
It's a treat that can't go wrong!

October 2024

JAVAID AND UZMA

Ham and eggs with whole wheat bread,
I'm about to break my fast.
Plated and served with garnish as trim,
The best of my daily repasts.

Once was a cook with recipe books,
And managed to succeed 'n' thrive.
But ran out of luck, competing with Puck,
Then knew I could never survive.

I regret I mistook, a chef for a cook,
Creating dishes with exotic themes.
For it's easier to sup, meals that sound nice,
Than dishes of limited means.

Lost to the craft are the condiments splashed,
That give food their color and taste.
To the last drop is the worthiest of tropes,
To recall whenever there's waste.

I'm retired now with little to share,
I've taken to nap on my bed.
I'm helped by Javaid every morning and night,
And have Uzma's omelets for breakfast instead.

November 2024

B.C.

Eons before the birth of Christ,
And hope restored on Earth.
Most people lived and died,
Uncertain of their worth.

Did they benefit from Christ's sacrifice,
Was salvation meant for all?
Was the yardstick made shorter,
To accommodate them all.

Or would they continue in disfavor,
Weighed by different scales.
Was limbo their only prospect,
Or oblivion and travail.

Believed in a higher being,
But still were prone to sin.
Created strange religions,
To slake the yen within.

Gods with animal features,
Pot-bellied Gods in stone.
Golden idols from the kiln,
And totems erect alone.

Some creeds had a tinge of truth,
Others in disrepute.
Temples with hellish rites,
And love forever moot.

For millennia they struggled,
Gradually improving their lot.
With truth still elusive,
It was something time forgot.

But the true God is always faithful,
And His promises He keeps.
Tho long suffering and patient,
These were souls He meant to reap.

Never would He abandon His children,
These were seeds He once had sown.
In mercy He would free them,
And make them again His own.

How He would accomplish this,
Is anybody's guess.
But since He's love and all-powerful,
He could do nothing less.

September 2022

ANOTHER ANGLE

Impressed on Him a crown of thorns,
To ridicule His claim.
Buffeted and scourged Him,
To intensify His pain.

Vested Him in purple cloth,
Enflaming those who came.
Enthroned Him on a crooked tree,
And held Him up to shame.

Despite sacrilege 'n' outrage,
He shouldered all their blame.
For millennia before Him,
And in future just the same.

An innocent as a newborn babe,
A sacrificial lamb.
Willingly sacrificed to set men free,
To mollify I AM.

Suffered sorely 'n' died for us,
To rise and live again.
Give us the key to heaven's gate,
God so loved the world of men.

August 2024

EGO TE ABSOLVO

Spotless as a newborn,
Once te absolvo is said.
A soul stained 'n' troubled,
Is pardoned now instead.

Free now to dine,
On divinity's spread.
Partake of the Eucharist,
That appears as if it's bread.

The soul is indeed happy,
To sup on such a meal.
Born of His goodness,
And His Passion's ordeal.

Neither faux nor fiction,
Or a contrarian's reveal.
But God's only Son,
Whose presence is real.

One step closer to Heaven,
Is he who subsists.
On His Body and Blood,
And all evil resists.

In Latin or English,
It means all the same.
The forgiveness of sins,
In the Trinity's name.

August 2024

GOOD FOOD

Invitations to the many,
For a celestial rendezvous.
Sup at heaven's table,
To partake of what ensues.

Choice fare from the valley,
Elixir from the vine.
To celebrate the Shepherd,
Who called His flock to dine.

Pastured them in the meadows,
Grazed them on the hills.
Gave us all His flesh to eat,
In keeping with God's will.

Those who trim their lanterns,
Clad spotlessly in white.
Find safety in the sheep cote,
Once hidden from their sight.

Joy awaits the many,
Who harkened to the Lamb.
Eternally glorified in sacrifice,
The Son – within I AM.

July 2024

ANGELS

Just a step or two behind me,
Hear a whisper in my ear.
Feel a tap upon my shoulders,
To assure me he's still here.

A sentinel with a halo,
With a yardstick as a rule.
A scale to weigh my actions,
With a conscience as a tool.

A twinge when he's compromised,
Guilt when he's ignored.
Harmonious in agreement,
For freedom and rapport.

A feather as a counterweight,
That perfection be assured.
A life-long companion,
So impurities be removed.

Two angels on my shoulders,
A red one with a tine.
A trope for a pitchfork,
To tempt and to malign.

The other in heavenly raiment,
To protect me with his sword.
Dispatch evil, when it rears its head,
As the champion of the Lord.

July 2024

A POINT OF VIEW

Where Second House Road,
And the Old Highway meet.
Lies a bit of heaven,
With only six streets.

There's a left turn to Gosman's,
Where old salts still ply.
East and West roads,
We drive by and by.

A lighthouse of stature,
Red, white and black.
A point of reflection,
To forestall any wrecks.

Big yachts and trawlers,
For the deepest of seas.
That reap nature's bounty,
To provide what we need.

There are sails on the pond,
Salt in the air.
Surf for the brave,
Bills of great fare.

A honky-tonk village,
For the haves and have-nots.
Where we love to go,
When the weather gets hot.

There are pristine beaches,
Upon which we lie.
And the pictures we imagine,
As the clouds pass us by.

The thoughts of leaving,
Bring tears to our eyes.
'Cause Montauk is special,
And you can only guess why!

June 2024

EFFULGENCE

Effulgent is God's glory,
An endless stream of light.
That reflects His very essence,
Tho' invisible to sight.

He's the Alpha and Omega,
The beginning and the end.
The I AM ever present,
Upon whom all depends.

He exudes love and mercy,
With a gift of purest joy.
Tho' silent in demeanor,
His Word He did deploy.

He enfleshed His Son to heal us,
And enrich impoverish souls.
Break the chains that bind us,
Make us pure and whole.

Redeemed us through His Passion,
Died and rose in three.
The innocent lamb of sacrifice,
Who survived the crooked tree.

Love is His motivation,
The God of three in One.
Who loved the world so much,
He sent His only Son.

June 2024

TIME

There is nothing left to ponder,
There is nothing more to say.
There's nowhere for me to wander,
There are no mere strings to play.

The days are getting longer,
Time is getting short.
The years get older faster,
Father Time is holding court.

The future once was distant,
But soon became the past.
Now is forever present,
Becoming later very fast.

Like the wind, it has no body,
Still time is passing by.
Taking a toll upon our bodies,
Unseen before our eyes.

Time, unfortunately, waits for no one,
It's a relic of the Fall,
Meant to fly throughout our lifetimes,
'Til there's no time left at all.

April 2024

LONGINUS

Don't know where I'm going,
Or recall where I've been.
Can't remember my beginning,
But believe there's no end.

How long has He loved me?
How long has it been?
Tho' He knew I'd betray Him,
By the deadliest of sins.

How drear was the day,
And the cruelty borne.
The barbarity 'n' suffering,
Before Easter morn.

Still hear the clamor,
The day He was betrayed.
The bearers of palms,
And hosannas in praise.

The bite of the flagellum,
The sting of the lash.
Nails to depend Him,
Distended to grasp.

I wince, too, at the spear thrust,
By Longinus of Rome.
Who pierced The Lamb's heart,
While softening his own.

Now washed in the lamb's blood,
In rue and regret.
Avowed Christ was God's Son,
And lost all respect.

But prompted by grace,
He followed his heart.
Becoming a saint,
Portrayed by chisel 'n' art.

And God in His wisdom,
Resolved the dilemma of Eden.
Accepting Christ's passion,
In behalf of His children.

March 2024

CRYSTAL BALL

I sit now by my window,
To see the world outside.
Lamb's wool in the ether,
Dead leaves flying by.

I'm older than the temperature,
Higher than outdoors.
Even in the dead of summer,
Seldom it is more.

The sun comes out, then goes in,
And when it rains, it pours.
Beating upon my windowpane,
Like someone at my door.

My salad days come to mind,
When the green meant something more.
When we thought we knew our destiny,
Yet, the future we ignored.

I'm glad 'n' sad I've come so far,
As the world contracts in size.
Now I let my mind do all the work,
And no longer exercise.

Then is now and that too will pass,
As time goes flying by.
Watch lambkins romp 'n' play,
'Til they dissipate and die.

Magic is my window,
It's a big world after all.
'Cause my imagination takes me everywhere,
As befits a crystal ball.

March 2024

SHORT CUTS

Violet are the sunsets,
Rosy are the dawns.
In between the twilight,
The dim ere dusk 'n' dawn.

The shine within the daytime,
The gray before the storm.
The rain upon the garden,
The snow beyond the norm.

Hands are rubbed when colder,
Brows are wiped when warm.
Stroll among the daisies,
Leaves raked when summer's gone.

Turkeys in the oven,
Pumpkins on the sill.
Gourmands at the table,
A fire for the chill.

Rosy pink awaiting,
A star ahead at night.
A family in a stable,
The god-man born of light.

Trees bedecked in glory,
Gifts below in box and bow.
A time for love 'n' family,
Windowed candles all aglow.

Once new, but getting older,
On a Happy New Year's day,
Popping corks to hear the bubbles,
Raise the glass 'n' yell hurray.

A card for a beloved,
Chocolate candies in a box.
A ring to hold 'em steady,
Just the thought, not the rock.

The paraders on St. Patrick's,
The wearing of the green.
A few shots before, to stem the cold,
Before shamrocks are ever seen.

Waving fronds a prelude,
To The Messiah's final meal.
The gift of His very essence,
By a miracle surreal.

Sup for a baker's dozen,
Bread without the yeast.
Wine within a body,
For a sacramental feast.

We cross our minds with ashes,
To recall the day forlorn.
The day He died for everyone,
Before He was reborn.

Walked the Earth for 40 days,
To answer all the doubters.
"My Lord 'n' My God," then went home,
With this avowal being shouted.

So around and on, the years add-up,
    'Til there's nothing more to say.
Then all's left to do, is hit the scales,
And be weighed on judgement day.

March 2024

SLEEPLESS

My wink is gone,
I'm beat and worn.
My mind's amok,
So I'm exhausted by dawn.

My head can't sleep,
It's screwed on wrong.
Bedeviled by thoughts,
That arrive like a storm.

I twist and turn,
In search of a nook.
Where off I can nod,
By hook or by crook.

Try as I may,
I stay open-eyed.
Tho' the lids are closed,
That cover my eyes.

Perhaps it's these rhymes,
That run through the night.
That keep me awake,
With little respite.

Loathe to take pills,
But something must give.
For being forever a zombie,
Is no way to live.

March 2024

COLOR-BLIND

Long may it wave,
Said the son of a slave.
Who served with distinction,
When the flag was engaged.

In a color-blind war,
Bullets don't care.
The color of victims,
As they whiz through the air.

Standing tall in courage,
In response to one's heart.
Is all that matters,
When asked to take part.

Color doesn't prevail,
When engaged in a fight.
But bravery 'n' loyalty,
Morality and might.

All should respond,
To a clarion call.
For as an immigrant nation,
We're one or we fall.

Sundry are wars,
The enemy diverse.
Outside or inside,
Perhaps even worse.

All merit our unity,
No heritage averse.
For wars are divisive,
And divinely accursed.

March 2024

CONNECTIONS

An ampersand seems an ancient symbol,
A rune upon a wall.
A curse to bewitch the unwary,
A hex to bring misfortune to all.

More benign than the ill-begotten,
Meant to conjoin two thoughts as one.
In lieu of an and, used to expand,
A grammatical duet like a rhyme.

The word, too, is the same by design,
With some ahead 'n' others behind.
Elaborates on the subject in question,
Making one from two of a kind.

Opposites attract is the wisdom,
Like heaven or hell, and water and wine.
Words with contrary meanings,
Still joined at the hip by a sign.

Also, we embellish a meaning,
With no need to parse or to spell.
Just to share whatever's in mind,
Like a bucket in an ol' wishing well.

A curlicue bent round with a flair,
Like a banjo strummed on demand.
A connecting link that makes us think,
An ampersand is merely a nine-lettered and.

February 2024

CARDBOARD BOXES

On the street without a pillow,
Cardboard boxes for their bed.
Debris amidst the discards,
Children lie where vermin fed.

Waifs so long abandoned,
Much deprived with little gain.
Seek a measure of compassion,
Safe alee against the grain.

Lacking love and affection,
Sought to find a better life.
Misled by the world's deceptions,
Happenstance to bitter strife.

Desperate for assistance,
Something warm, a piece of bread.
A selfless hand, a little succor,
No more fear but love instead.

Some survive, some don't make it,
What a shame, who's to blame.
Indeed, that's the proverbial question,
Posed to all who work in vain.

Perhaps the better remedy,
Is to refer to The One who knows.
Unerring in His judgement,
Than the experts at work below.

February 2024

THE HOLY GRAIL

Said to be of polished Sardis,
Is the vessel that we seek.
That slaked our thirst at the last repast,
As The Word was said to speak.

A cup of blood His wine became,
After bread possessed Him whole.
The Holy Grail Galahad sought,
To mend our wayward souls.

A chalice rare that we might share,
In heaven's holy grace.
Now some believe it's in filigreed gold,
In a discrete and holy place.

Where might it be the cup we seek,
The Good Lord only knows.
Be assured it's within our grasp,
But where, they'll not disclose.

Three in Spain do assert the claim,
And their provenance they'll gladly share.
That theirs is the one that touched His lips,
And had salvation brought to bear.

On the final day we'll know for sure,
When He parts the goats and sheep.
Toasts those who overcame life's storms,
With the cup, we need no longer seek.

February 2024

THE WIND

Under the guise of the seen 'n' unseen,
There's an invisible force we feel.
A current of air with tres savoir-faire,
Unseen, but never-the-less real.

A colorless chameleon in flight,
That travels incognito at night.
'Til unannounced bedevils the dust,
And gives us a sense of its might.

It often bends trees to its will,
Yet an imperceptible breeze when still.
A gust of air that ruffles one's hair,
Offing hats, to fly where they will.

Enraged when it comes in a roar,
Cyclonic when it scours the shore.
Spins on high to darken the sky,
When spent, drops to the floor.

At the wheel of an oft' driven snow,
Reshapes all the deserts we know.
Vests every ocean in white caps,
And fills sails of barques as they go.

In fact, where does it go when it goes?
Just God and His wind only know.
A relief when hot, colder when not,
A fan of nature, whenever she blows.

February 2024

THE PLAZA

Palms hold court at The Plaza,
Where Eloise is recalled with a smile.
The elegant appear in their finery,
And its rooms are the epitome of style.

A jewel in the crown of the city,
With a fountain and Bergdorf nearby.
Poster child of the Big Apple,
From an orchard that many admire.

Its Clam Bar is the epicure's haven,
A fish house that's tucked out of sight.
Ideal for afternoon trysts,
And a great place to stop for a bite.

Neighbor to horse 'n' carriage,
That travel at a tedious pace.
Make it 'round Central Park by bedtime,
With horses that lose every race.

The source of so many memories,
Our annual family soiree.
Christmas time in the Eloise suite,
With room service at the end of the day.

With fairytale lights in the skyline,
A stroll down Fifth Avenue at night.
A visit to St. Patrick's Cathedral,
Then Rock Center 'n' all its delights.

The Christmas tree resplendent in glory,
Silver blades flashing on ice.
A gold Prometheus, the god of fire,
Offering skaters an experts' advice.

A magical tour for a family,
A unique and memorable respite.
An experience we often relive,
When we celebrate Christmas night.

February 2024

THE PURPLE

Invested in the purple,
Are kings and priests alike.
The sovereigns in suzerainty,
Priests in Lenten rite.

Kings wield the scepter,
Priests a piece of bread.
Vested at the altar,
Kings enthroned instead.

Both are blessed with oils,
On assumption of their roles,
Commit to royal service,
To make their people whole.

Divine right is their license,
The essence of their reign.
Authorized by heaven,
To serve The Holy Name.

Long a royal color,
A symbol of their rights.
Kings rule upon the earth,
Priests pray for one's rebirth.

Both will stand before the Lord,
At the end we're all the same.
See who best wears the purple,
And deserves eternal fame.

January 2024

INCENSE

Rising on high, lost to our eyes,
Incense carries our prayers to God.
Speaks to our ills, in accord with His will,
As quick as a wink and a nod.

Sweet fragrant pleas, oft' from our knees,
Offers, too, thanksgiving and praise.
Tho' He already knows our joys 'n' our woes,
He still awaits what we wish to convey.

It lingers as haze, as we consider our ways,
And the ritual beginning before us.
When the Lord's body 'n' blood revisits the altar,
Appearing common but ever glorious.

Like sweet smelling nard, a scent from the heart,
Incense formalizes the homage we pay.
To an Almighty God who gifts what we have,
Ours, 'til the end of our days.

Let it waft on the breeze, o'er land 'n' the seas,
Spread its fragrance far 'n' wide.
Showing the world, it's His after all,
And by His Word we should always abide.

January 2024

OUTER SPACE

Light years beyond the firmament,
Where His workshop 'n' space converge.
God tinkers with creation,
And galaxies 'n' nebulae emerge.

Like pearls on black velvet,
That enhances their luster 'n' shine.
Overcomes the drear of chaos,
With divinity's unique design.

His mind is eternally fertile,
Is The God of love and surprise.
Fashioning worlds from nothing,
To mesmerize prying eyes.

Some appear benign and amorphous,
One a disinterred hand.
Another a string of diamonds,
An hourglass sifting sand.

A trumpet to acknowledge His glory,
Cymbals that respond to The Word.
Timbrels that echo their praises,
Gasses that appear as a bird.

Their beauty has no equal,
Except for the creation of man.
Made in The Father's image,
When humanity first began.

The curious search for answers,
Scouring space and its art.
When the answer to the existential question,
May be found in the depths of their hearts.

January 2024

WAIFS

Deign do I, ponder and cry,
O'er waifs in consternation.
In want of bread and a place for their heads,
While in the throes of tribulations.

Often they scream silent screams,
To voice their fears 'n' frustrations.
Hoping Lady justice will open her eyes,
And notice their deprivation.

Fair or no, few or many,
They plead for recognition.
A sip of water 'n' a crust of bread,
Would improve their disposition.

Remote are we from the carnage we see,
Indifferent to their situation.
Deaf to their cries, cause most to surmise,
We can't remedy their desperation.

The generous come forth and do what they ought,
To work for their liberation.
Succor their ills, tend to their spills,
And allay the effects of starvation.

Intercession and one's compassion,
Are keys to their salvation.
In keeping with, the man on a tree,
Who died for their resurrection.

December 2023

THE BREAD OF LIFE

O House of Bread, of thee' it's said,
Your inn should have more rooms.
Having relegated Him, who makes all things,
To a stable, cave and gloom.

The last resort to secure a bed,
Barely apt for one to stay.
Let alone bear a child,
To whom the world would pray.

Born was He to a lady fair,
The immaculate still is she.
Born herself in God's good grace,
As pure and chase as He.

A tableau of love and beauty,
A picture of peace and grace.
A Christmas scene to remember,
A babe in her embrace.

Bathed in light and angel song,
A star and glory be.
Reconciled man to God,
Seeing Him, The Son in three.

Christmas wreathes 'n' twinkling lights,
Gifts beneath the tree.
Fail to measure up to The Son of God,
For The Bread of Life is He.

December 2023

OXYMORON

Much is spent to circumvent,
The end of life on Earth.
Seeking a source of life in space,
To give humankind new birth.

Scientific discoveries 'n' medical marvels,
Skills that help us mend.
Foster health to prolong our lives,
Upon which longevity depends.

Thankful are we for the genius we see,
Cures that warm the heart.
That succor our ills, in accord with God's will,
With the heavenly gifts He imparts.

While many contend life is their end,
They treat the living with hate 'n' disdain.
From social squabbles to misguided quarrels,
To acts that maim and enflame.

From the unborn to the war-torn,
They distance themselves from pain.
Believing one's plight is their misfortune,
As they sanitize themselves from blame.

Justified by catchy slogans,
Rights precedent to inflicted pain.
We continue to kill with impunity,
Impervious to the concordant shame.

December 2023

A CHRISTMAS NAP

Snuggled by the fire,
With a blanket on my lap.
That befits an older body,
About to take a nap.

Didn't sleep a wink last night,
So my eyes began to close.
My eyelids dropped as the flames flared up,
As I slid into repose.

Like a Currier and Ives Christmas card,
Graced with falling snow.
Safe from the throes of winter,
Aside a fire's glow.

Heard carols in the distance,
Wassailing on a sleigh.
Reminded me of the early years,
And home on Christmas Day.

Dreamt of exotic places,
Places far away.
But home is where my heart is,
So here I plan to stay.

Blest I've been o'er the years,
Through many ups and downs.
But always feel peace and joy,
When Christmas comes around.

December 2023

CHRISTMAS CHILD

There's a baby in the manger,
That looks to be my friend.
Arrives with no beginning,
And leaves without an end.

See Him once a year at Christmas,
When the trees are dressed in white.
As nature sings peace on earth,
On the holiest of nights.

Never grows old from year to year,
Receives visitors with delight.
Insists on playing with a wooden cross,
In the silence of the night.

Tho' He be small; He made us all,
Sleeps in a stable, as we know.
A cave swept clean of dung 'n' dross,
As the cattle kneel and low.

O holy child, may we too stay small,
And extend our arms like you.
Be held fast to your tiny breast,
And be assured your love's secure.

Born into time on Christmas Day,
To save mankind from sin.
O child sublime, O Babe divine,
Be merciful when the end begins.

December 2023

HOT AIR

Diogenes canvased Athens,
Seeking an honest man.
With lantern in hand, found no such man,
As he expected, when he first began.

Honesty is rare, due to the sin we bear,
That weakens conscience 'n' soul.
Which leads to poor choices 'n' discordant voices,
Levying an exorbitant toll.

So we see evil run free and crime on a spree,
Poisoning the American Dream.
Plagued with civil disorder 'n' irrational schemes,
We risk coming apart at the seams.

We've touted too long the melting pot thesis,
When we're a mosaic with different pieces.
Tho' many buy-in, too many dig-in,
Too set in their ways for syntheses.

A house divided cannot stand,
And still believe they're a unified nation.
For self-interest prevails, no matter who fails,
Filled with acrimony and dissention.

With the Decalog considered an outdated guide,
And God's name banished when the public's speaking.
It appears we've sanctioned our own demise,
Preferring hot air to eternal teaching.

Woke is a joke; biology's not broke,
Pray sanity is restored to our nation.
Truth sets us free and will ever be,
The way to our country's salvation.

November 2023

THE CROWNING

Twas' a crown in heaven's closet,
Ablaze as a comet's tail.
Reserved for a special lady,
Who would elicit our prayers and hail.

Awaited the birth of a maiden,
A sinless and immaculate lass.
Who merited God's favor,
When the nativity came to pass.

Responded to an angel's greeting,
Said "yes" to enflesh God's Son.
Would be the beginning of Salvation History,
To mend what our parent had done.

Undefiled then and forever,
The beneficiary of singular grace.
Overshadowed by The Holy Spirit,
The pride of the human race.

Nurtured Him in His childhood,
Held Him fast in time 'n' space.
Was proud of His every endeavor,
Saddened as they marred His face.

Stood by Him when sorely afflicted,
Wept bitterly when nailed to a tree.
Distraught at His suffering 'n' death,
Overjoyed when resurrected 'n' free.

Empowered with tongues of fire,
Upon whom the Apostles depend.
Would counsel the nascent church,
'Til she fell asleep at the end.

The Apostles would weep at her dormition,
With the loss of mother and friend.
Interred her in accord with tradition,
Overwhelmed when alive once again.

For she would be assumed to the highest heaven,
Beyond where meteors run.
Then crowned with the headpiece in the closet,
By a grateful and loving Son.

Now eternally the Queen of Heaven,
The intercessor for all our pleas.
Preconceived by the Holy Trinity,
Their most generous 'n' glorious deed.

November 2023

FORGIVEN

Hailed with palms 'n' praises,
Reviled upon a hill.
Betrayed by chosen people,
Who chose to have Him killed.

Raucous crowds assailed Him,
Hearts of stone prevailed.
Hosannas long forgotten,
For a victim impaled with nails.

Miracles notwithstanding,
Those raised again to life.
The lepers 'n' the blind He cured,
Was subjected to the strife.

Unforgiving was His Passion,
Agony dogged His every step.
Yet forgave each and every one,
Complicit in His death.

His body was cruelly treated,
A body death would claim.
But rose again three days hence,
To glory and acclaim.

The Prince of Peace, The King of Kings,
Now sits upon His throne.
Working still as The Father wills,
To invite His people home.

November 2023

SCALING THE MOUNTAIN

I hope to climb the mountain,
One faces when we die.
Criss-crossed with sundry burdens,
Impediments to reach the prize.

Boulders of pride and envy,
Stones of injustice and greed.
Concupiscence and dishonesty,
And other nefarious deeds.

Sins against life and gluttony,
Escarpments and unstable screes.
That cause us to slip and stumble,
Bloodying spiritual knees.

The crevices, too, are daunting,
A challenge to misguided creeds.
Acts of commission 'n' omission,
That suggest that we do as we please.

One hopes they've availed of God's mercy,
No matter the trespass perceived.
Thread the eye of the needle,
To achieve what God had decreed.

The view from the top is glorious,
God and mansions galore.
With all the doors wide open,
No fear of thieves anymore.

November 2023

THE TRAVELER

I hear the train a-coming,
Clickety-clack around the bend.
Soon will hear the wheels a-screeching,
As it comes to journey's end.

The conductor's bailing out a door,
The engineer's loyal guide.
To bring her home smoothly,
Along the platform's side.

Some come out and some go in,
As I'm waiting for my turn.
I don't know where I'm going,
But traveling is what I yearn.

I've scrimped and saved my money,
And have some vittles in my pouch.
I just want to see the world,
As I have from grandma's couch.

I'm a traveler by nature,
And I'm tired of picking corn.
The corn is mighty pretty,
But I've been picking since I'm born.

I know Ma and Pa will miss me,
When they discover that I'm gone.
Call the sheriff for assistance,
Spread the word with great alarm.

Left a note in the woodshed,
Where Pa goes every morn.
Told him not to worry,
Nor for Mom to feel forlorn.

Tell Mary Sue I love her,
And I'll write from where I've gone.
I'll tell her of my adventures,
As I recall our favorite song.

Perhaps then I'll join the army,
Where the clothes n' food are free.
Tell them I'm from Ol' Kentucky,
Ol' Dan'l Boone and me.

Then I plan to go to Europe,
Paris, France and then to Rome.
Explore all the sites at leisure,
Before I leave and head on home.

We'll all be a lot grayer then,
And the trees will have more rings.
Hope Mary Sue will love my wife,
Cause she's deadly with a sling.

So, I'll be a little cautious,
And send a telegram instead.
For in the wisdom of Confucius,
Better alive than dead.

November 2023

THE SPIRIT

The Spirit gives us life,
He whispers in our ears.
Animates the soul within,
The inspirations that we hear.

Appearing as a Dove,
But unlikely that above.
A bond between the other two,
The ultimate exchange of love.

A patron of the arts,
The talent He imparts.
To those that wield the brush,
And sonnets from the heart.

He breaths in us new life,
Makes us pure and clean.
Empowers us with fiery tongues,
Our lover though unseen.

Eternal God is He,
The God that lets us be.
One with those who creates us all,
The Holy God of Three.

We offer Him our prayers,
In the hope that we might share.
A modicum of the grace we need,
To partake of heaven's fare.

November 2023

MARTYRDOM

Blood of martyrs,
Seeds of the bride.
Born of The Word,
So His church would survive.

An eternity of bliss,
Await those who believe.
Broadcast the faith,
So the truth be received.

Shed their blood,
Out of conviction 'n' love.
Followed their Lord,
Who reigns now above.

Supreme was the sacrifice,
Many endured.
Unspeakable horrors,
So the faith be secured.

First of the martyrs,
Who offered their lives.
Preceded the many,
Who followed and died.

Their precious blood,
Forever esteemed.
Great the reward,
That souls be redeemed.

October 2023

RISE

Yeast plumps the dough to make it grow,
See it rise before our eyes.
Oven-baked 'til golden brown,
Crusty loaves of every size.

"The Staff of Life" its claim to fame,
Enough to be a meal.
From ages past, 'twas made to last,
Be it whole or just a heel.

"The Bread of Life," a simile,
Offers an eternity of bliss.
Transubstantiated by its maker,
For an appearance such as this.

Small 'n' round, the divine is found,
Jesus Christ, the prize.
A mysterious 'n' miraculous recipe,
Becomes His flesh 'n' blood inside.

Unleavened without the yeast,
Hidden from our very eyes.
Tho' the taste is bland, at His command,
Only He can make us rise.

October 2023

AT THE MOVIES

The picture finally ended,
"Finis" said so on the screen.
The credits started rolling,
As they replayed the movie's theme.

Stragglers finished their popcorn,
Most stormed the theater's doors.
The critics were unanimous,
The worst they ever saw.

The story was a drama,
A comedy of sorts.
A biography of a mirror,
Reflecting all its warts.

Often times a sinner,
A time or two a saint.
Most times you or me,
Noting each complaint.

A comedy of errors,
A cast without a name.
Not a formula for an Oscar,
A Divine Comedy just the same.

September 2023

AN AUTUMNAL VISION

Beyond the dell where acorns fell,
And scampering squirrels dine.
Leaves of gold descend en masse,
To celebrate pumpkin time.

Softly drop like wafts of white,
Rise with gusts and blows.
Carpet the ground of a tree's surround,
Until chased by the driven snow.

A picture framed in Autumn's name,
A pastiche of red and gold.
A glorious display of an artist's hand,
That fades when days grow cold.

Time for the hearth and a family round,
A toddy laced with rum.
Or a shandy spiked with brandy,
Bales of hay and purple mums.

An admiring ride in the countryside,
Sees nature at its very best.
Brilliant leaves amid needles of green,
That will be seen when the trees undress.

The scent of air, sweet and rare,
Reminds all of the feasts to come.
When the meals of the season exceed all reason,
And eaten to the very last crumb.

September 2023

WITNESS OF NATURE

Impressive the sky when it rumbles and cries,
With bundles of lamb's wool when it's blue and it's dry.
Leaves that rustle on branches of trees,
Fields at attention golden in sheaves.

Droplets from heaven harbingers of rain,
Streams aflow and parting in twain.
Wheat and tares that grow side by side,
Oceans that fall and rise with the tides.

Spheres of the firmament that rotate at will,
We also revolve while the sun's standing still.
Stars who beguile us ever so bright,
Cast cross the heavens to guide us at night.

The glory of nature in witness to Him,
Confirms His creation born of His whim.
Long in His being, always in mind,
Myriad creatures, a diversity of kind.

Birds of a feather, birds on the wing,
Feathered songbirds created to sing.
Four legged ruminants that run like the wind,
Their beauty beheld in thunder 'n' din.

Snow-capped escarpments precipiced steep,
Peaks in ascendence with falls seen to weep.
Trenches in oceans darker than deep,
Sliding tectonics that slip while we sleep.

What about man and his neighbor next door,
Made in His image so God be adored.
Why can't we believe that which we see,
Made for our pleasure most times for free.

All bespeak of an all-knowing God,
Who many doubt and others think odd.
The day will arrive when one looks to survive,
Only to find, it's His spirit that keeps us alive.

September 2023

CASTING STONES

They skim along the surface,
Stones cast across the pond.
A wake amid the ripples,
Three daps before they're gone.

Just a game for children,
When there's little else to do.
Dislodge a frog from a lily pad,
To hear a croak or two.

Scale a rock to see it drop,
As it plops into the green.
Scattering bugs on the pad next door,
Meant for the night's cuisine.

Google-eyed it hides behind,
A lily pad in bloom.
Waiting for the kid to leave,
So its nap it might resume.

August 2023

HEAVENLY BUSINESS

Jesus, O Savior, twas our behavior,
That caused you such rancor 'n' pain.
Saw you arise after being demised,
Escorted to your heavenly reign.

A body ablaze transcendent in ways,
Bright as the noonday sun.
Pleased His father in front of His mother,
When He said the Messiah had won.

The Word from above, the embodiment of love,
Was enfleshed by an innocent maiden.
Held tight to her breast, then, and at last,
When joyful or heavily laden.

Can't comprehend, the cruelty of men,
That finds pleasure in irrational treatment.
Far less than He, who caused them to be,
And finds glee in God's abasement.

Betrothed to a church often besmirched,
With sacraments to never deceive us.
Gave us His mother, pure like no other,
A God who eternally conceived us.

She'll come to our aid, as many have bade,
To enter the halls of heaven.
Fights for what's right, well into the night,
When rising needs a pinch of leaven.

August 2023

THE KINGDOM

An everlasting kingdom,
Ancient when new.
An indecipherable mystery,
Known to be true.

Invisible yet present,
Here but unseen.
Just but merciful,
The divinity's scheme.

Home to pure spirits,
Who fly on command.
Up to a higher heaven,
To accommodate man.

The Almighty's perfect,
But creation not so.
To separate Him,
From all that we know.

His gift of election,
Has the gap grow.
Betrayed the villain,
That caused it be so.

Some angels chose war,
An apple lured man.
Disobedient by degree,
Both became damned.

Yet, God was merciful,
That man be consoled.
Was given a new chance,
To again be made whole.

August 2023

EGYPTIAN

O Pharoah, My Pharoah,
Scabbard your sword.
Don not your armor,
We've reached an accord.

Our steeds have been stabled,
Our chariots stilled.
They've taken a knee,
And will submit to your will.

Their flag seeking parlay,
Still flies from yon hill.
Their leader chastened,
Who thought to do ill.

Half their army's now carrion,
Half ran away.
A rout of an army,
That abandoned the fray.

Your victory, Pharoah, we will remember,
And your deeds we'll recall.
Inscribed for posterity,
On all Karnack's walls.

Maat, too, has recovered,
And your Ka soon adored.
The old gods revered,
As a result of your sword.

In time culture will change,
And its Gods fade away.
A Great one will appear,
Then Rome's eagle hold sway.

Egypt will forever be glorious,
Even though in museums.
Mummified for the ages,
To share sages' dreams.

August 2023

A CHARCOAL FIRE

I see in the distance,
A sail that's unfurled.
Riding the crest,
Of a sun-dappled world.

A vessel of grace,
Traversing the sea.
Sailing in silence,
On a puff to alee.

Appeared to be gliding,
On the glassiest of seas.
Becoming more violent,
As it flows nigh to me.

Carries a treasure,
Cargoed on board.
Destined for souls,
Seeking The Lord.

Crewed by twelve angels,
Winged to soar.
Forestalled flotsam 'n' jetsam,
From reaching the shore.

There He awaits,
Stoking a fire.
Grilling choice fishes,
For our delight 'n' desire.

August 2023

VAGARIES OF WAR

The armada opened fire,
With a salvo of shells.
Greeting an island,
With an aloha from hell.

Bright red plumes,
Preceded their sounds.
And hot yellow tracers,
Spread lead all around.

They lit up the beaches,
And leveled the ground.
Expecting a cakewalk,
But cake never found.

Marines hit the beaches,
Tho' not easily endured.
The resistance was daunting,
Not a cakewalk for sure.

Everyone was frightened,
Everyone scared.
All tense 'n' anxious,
No one was spared.

Casualties and losses,
Exceeded what the brass thought.
Reinforcements were necessary,
To spell those who fought.

Victory was garnered,
After months on the line.

Tho' the enemy was determined,
To charge one more time.

The body count repelled,
Those keeping score.
Who counted the dog tags,
And the names that they bore.

The flag upright in victory,
A clear sign we won.
But the horrors of battle,
Stained everyone.

The incessant rains inland,
The ankle-deep mud.
Malaria and dysentery,
The filth and the crud.

The death of a buddy,
The cries and the moans.
The appeals to heaven,
And to mothers back home.

How do we convey this,
To all future sons.
The futility of war,
When we again need our guns.

For our enemies today,
May be tomorrow our friends.
Former allies our enemies,
'Til we've exhausted these trends.

So pray to The Lord,
That His reign will begin.
That plow shares will be relevant,
With neither war and nor sin.

July 2023

MANSIONS OF THE LORD

To our fallen comrades let us sing,
Who served our country 'til death's sting.
Their broken bodies let us bring,
To the mansions of The Lord.

Where there's no more sorrow and no more pain,
No more fear of death in vain.
Heroes all may we proclaim,
To the mercy of The Lord.

Wore ID tags and body bags,
Now don the robes the holy wear.
Martyr's crowns the brave now bear,
In the mansions of The Lord.

Where no one cries,
And no one weeps.
Where love 'n' joy are theirs to keep,
Where angels lie and heroes sleep,
In the mansions of The Lord.

Now they serve a higher reign,
Warriors in the Lord's domain.
Where just Divine grace, eternal light pertain,
In the mansions of The Lord.

July 2023

Revised lyrics to the hymn from the Mel Gibson movie,
"We Were Soldiers," released in 2002.

DISCERNMENT

Some quake and fear,
The prospect we face.
The end of our years,
In applause or disgrace.

Should be honored instead,
To be a thought in His mind.
As a part of creation,
And the passage of time.

Asked that we live.
So we might return,
To an eternity of bliss,
Or whatever we've earned.

So simple it's hard,
To follow His plan.
Laid out before us,
To choose out of hand.

We can joyfully go up,
Or unhappily go down.
But we can't go both ways,
To reach holy ground.

If we only understood,
What it meant to be spurned,
We could have avoided the heat,
But, now, it's too late to learn.

July 2023

THE DOOR

I seek the door to evermore,
That portal in my soul.
That bids me knock to enter in,
To find the prize foretold.

It lies deep within my heart,
Where the Spirit of God abides.
And where flesh 'n' blood create,
A sanguine path inside.

It admits us to a kingdom,
A realm of joy and bliss.
An eternity with a compassionate God,
Where love and mercy kiss.

Redemption's door readily welcomes,
The reborn and contrite.
Where the truth softens stony hearts,
Evoking God's delight.

One day we'll stand before The Lord,
God's Son and final Word.
Confident of the promises made,
In every psalm we've heard.

They speak of God's mercy,
And the paradise we enjoyed before.
Ready to open at every knock,
To those who find the door.

July 2023

PILATE

Why, if any, have so many,
Acknowledged an infamous name.
Whose acclaim and notoriety,
Rose from hypocrisy and shame.

Cited frequently by worshipers,
Recalled the villainy displayed.
Believe his victim resurrected,
As He did Easter Day.

Pontius Pilate, history's villain,
The Roman who then held sway.
First demurred then condemned Him,
To His followers' dismay.

Hardly a paragon of virtue,
Who questioned what was true.
Washed his hands to deny the blame,
Seeking praise from Rome and Jew.

A pariah and denier,
Who hung Christ upon a tree.
Could still look to His mercy,
And have his soul set free.

His soul belongs to God alone,
So we should not judge or demean.
'Cause the ocean of God's mercy,
May have washed him clean.

July 2023

SUNSET

O beauty fair the heavens share,
Before dusk bedims the light.
Glory's mantle clads the sun,
Ere it goes to sleep at night.

An amber sky fleecy bright,
Casts its glow in flight.
Calls to mind the Master's brush,
That paints the scene each night.

Whisps of violet, a tinge of pink,
Streaks of mauve and gray.
Bands of gold in brilliant stripes,
Ends each summer day.

Rolling waves reflect the scene,
As they make their rippled way.
And the ocean gleams when rosy beams,
Touch the seas at play.

A celestial miracle we're blessed to see,
The Master's work at hand.
Watch it descend beneath the waves,
And reappear once more on land.

June 2023

GRAVY TRAIN

Went to the diner with three guys from China,
'cause he acquired a yen for their yen.
Corrupt and a liar, a shill and maligner,
The best of Delaware's men.

Worked out a deal, pursued with great zeal,
Believing no one would know.
But Hunter, the tout, had a big mouth,
And ten percent's a whole lot of dough.

With a little bit here 'n' a little bit there,
Bribes conveniently denied.
In queues by the score, the swamp looks for more,
Loves to make a bit on the side.

Joe may be considered an inept leader,
But has become the most successful of crooks.
Often lionized by a biased media,
Who ignores the money he took.

Nice to have a frugal first family,
Having multiple banks and accounts.
Who perfected passing the buck,
To launder significant amounts.

Thanksgiving must be especially generous,
A celebration that's one for the books.
'cause when someone asks for the gravy,
It's passed along by Hunter and not the cook!

June 2023

NIGHT JOURNEY

Wearied by a restless night,
I rub my eyes awake.
Can't recall the things I dreamt,
Despite the steps I take.

Sometimes cobwebs lose their touch,
And allow me to take a peek.
To see improbable places with unknown faces,
That we asleep might seek.

Perhaps prompted by my wasted years,
The unfulfilled dreams 'n' fears.
Bitter times and halcyon days,
My laughter or my tears.

They twist one's recall to make a point,
On a journey in travail.
For other outcomes have long since paled,
Prey to exotic tales.

Failures and successes with similar stresses,
Enhanced by chance 'n' degree.
Also, may serve to fantasize conclusions,
Decrying reality.

There must be a more peaceful way,
To spend the night and days.
Than to decipher the undecipherable,
That lead the mind astray.

Prayer offers an effective remedy,
A chat with Him as friend.
A relationship that lasts forever,
And never has an end.

It's certainly of greater value,
Than eerie and ungodly ways.
For its reward is everlasting,
And time ne'er comes into play.

So now I'm wed to a window seat,
With many thoughts to convey.
And as dusk arrives to reclaim the sky,
I sit alone and pray.

June 2023

AMERICA'S GAME

A cowhide round tightly wound,
Is central to this story.
Homeward bound 'till three are down,
Leads to angst or glory.

A man in black at a receiver's back,
Calls them as he sees 'em.
Balls and strikes to some dislike,
Depends on who believes him.

The game is played on emerald green,
With hits to sundry places.
Up and down, men go round,
Equi-distant bases.

Demands are voiced by rabid fans,
Seeking an advantage.
Take a chance, steal a base,
Somebody do some damage!

Frame after frame goes on the game,
Until all at-bats are outed.
Walk-off victories are especially prized,
And the batter highly touted.

The very best that pass the test,
End up in a shrine of glory.
They may be found in Cooperstown,
Where they'll end this baseball story.

June 2023

FROM ON HIGH

Long before the days of yore,
When the darkness was black 'n' deep.
If one could see, a spark they'd see,
Creation emerge from sleep.

Forever in the mind of the one Divine,
Expressed by God to be.
From joy to sorrow 'n' back again,
From an apple to a barren tree.

Absent time, in no time at all,
He became a creature enfleshed.
To save mankind from its Edenic fail,
Was born to a straw-lined creche.

God's very Word was broadcast 'n' heard,
By ears opened to hear.
Bathed in water and washed in blood,
Cured the blind and those diseased.

Wonders upon wonders astounded the needy,
As lepers and the dead could attest.
Yet hypocrites ignored tradition 'n' scripture,
And put the Messiah to death.

Beaten and scorned, pitifully forlorn,
Striped, scourged and flailed.
All to satisfy an incomparable debt,
Was depended by hammer 'n' nails.

Nobody talked the way He talked,
Nor walked the via the way He walked.
Burdened in grief with a sorrowful thief.
Sent a fragrant aroma to God.

Ominous clouds cowered the crowds,
The temple veil split aloud.
An innocent victim was sealed in a tomb,
Wrapped in a white linen shroud.

Sorrow and tears gripped Mother 'n' peers,
While His disciples scattered in fear.
Until that morn when a new world was born,
And the Christ from the creche reappeared.

"My Lord and My God," the doubter endowed,
And still echoes and resounds through the years.
For Christ is risen for the sake of His children,
And promised He'd always be here.

Now from on high, where mercy abides,
The Trinity need no longer hide.
'Cause the door to the kingdom has been reopened,
To permit the holy to eternally reside.

He'll return once again, when the Father says when,
To gather the lambs and the sheep.
But the goats He'll deny and forever condemn,
When one hears the gnashing of teeth.

May 2023

AN APPEAL

Long have l sought to knock at your door,
Your patience unending, your love evermore.
Knowing full well unworthy am I,
Still implore you sincerely to permit me inquire.

I try to conform my wants to your will,
Respond to your voice that calls to me still.
Follow the way for which you're the guide,
Suffer my crosses to vanquish my pride.

Venerate your name and share your pain,
One of The Trinity one and the same.
Your love is forever, eternal your reign,
I've sought your mercy again 'n' again.

O heavenly bliss, O heavenly sun,
Often disregarded by a recalcitrant one.
Known me forever 'n' all that I've done,
Trust new choices will comport with your Son.

Forever together in a dream I behold,
More vivid today 'cause I'm wizened 'n' old.
By faith I believe and in hope I aspire,
In charity I adore you before I expire.

O compassionate Savior, O compassionate Lord,
To live in joy and eternal accord.
You made me to save me, so I trust you'll succeed,
It's my fervent desire, as I fall to my knees.

May 2023

WALKING ON WATER

He walked on the Sea of Galilee,
A sea He once created.
Stilled the winds 'n' calmed the waters,
The Messiah long awaited.

Turned out He was, Who He said He was,
Avowing indeed it was He.
Gave them a hand 'n' led them to land,
The frightened 'n' imperiled at sea.

Row as they might all through the night,
Trying to reach Capernaum.
Fought the sea wave after wave,
In a gale well beyond them.

About to founder saw a figure,
Spectre-like in the distance.
Walking at ease on a turbulent sea,
With little or no resistance.

Calling aloud to his disciples on board,
Invited Peter to test the waters.
Extended His hand to a soon-sinking man,
Whose faith had wavered 'n' faltered.

"Get back on the boat 'n' nevermore doubt,
You who often denied me.
For I AM the way, the truth and the life,
And trust is required to serve me."

May 2023

ALMOST TOO LATE

Whither thou goest,
O disheartened soul.
Who walks in the shadow,
Too many extol.

A pathway to sorrow,
Enticed by bright lights.
That dim and sputter,
When needed at night.

A recall of the past,
Down memory lane.
Reveals poor choices,
For temporal gain.

Ignored every signpost,
Every plea that one heard.
Passed every by-way,
Dismissed every word.

Troubled by a conscience,
That winces and bites.
Warns of a judgement,
That has no respite.

Yet mercy awaits the pitiful soul,
Late to the party but finally made whole.
Truly contrite for grievous sin,
Now ever joyful and welcomed within.

May 2023

HE SAID....

I sought and found the master's door,
A door He asked I find.
Found deep within my soul,
And the recesses of my mind.

"Knock and enter in," He said,
I need do nothing more.
He'd greet me with open arms,
As promised years before.

"Ask and receive," He said,
As I held the door ajar.
"What might I receive, I asked,
It can't be very far.

Instead, saw angels pluck golden harps,
Fleecy clouds a glow.
Mountains high that pierced the sky,
In a heavenly tableau.

He stood there with open arms,
His wounded hands ablaze.
The most glorious sight ever seen,
Worthy of all praise.

"Believe in what I say," He said,
"Only say. What is true.
Trust in me to show the way,
And do what you should do."

Wonder whether that sufficed,
To justify my search.
Then revisited the tableau I saw,
And became committed to His Church.

April 2023

COMPASSION

They cower in the shadows,
Afraid they might offend.
Glean wasted fields for supper,
For which sustenance depends.

Fearful in the evening,
Frightened late at night.
Guarded in the we'est hours,
Hapless in morning's light.

Victims of pure happenstance,
Victims of their plight.
Can't recall a time of joy,
Fell prey to another's rights.

Never agreed to their existence,
Born without a say.
A simple accident of nature,
To stay or not to stay.

The dependent 'n' the lonely,
The homeless and the poor.
Begrimed by filth and circumstance,
A prison to be sure.

Just a sip of water,
Just a piece of cake.
To help desperate people,
That's all it really takes.

Just add a little compassion,
A sincere and helping hand.
An expression of togetherness,
To get them to rise 'n' stand.

April 2023

REGRETS

It was a sad day, a somber day,
A day they'd soon regret.
When small-minded men in black 'n' white,
Put The Christ to death.

Hoped to thwart the things He taught,
Fearful of what they'd seen.
Miracles performed on rich and poor,
Eroding their esteem.

Thought they'd be free by a tree,
But shocked n' surprised to see.
A risen Messiah alive again,
One of The Eternal Three.

To this day they assert in dismay,
His body was lifeless 'n' dead.
He never arose as some suppose,
Just a rumor His disciples spread.

Born, of course, to suffer the cross,
Freeing all from their sin 'n' dross.
Knowing full well He'd judge them one day,
To determine their gain or loss.

Pity the small who plotted the fall,
For theirs was a time to regret.
Never recalled what the prophets foretold,
A day they'll never forget.

April 2023

TIME CLOCK

A beautiful arbor embowered with flowers,
Appeared in the Spring again.
A creation of nature foreseen by Her maker,
Praised by a resounding Amen.

Her beauty bestowed 'n' gloriously clothed,
With roses and lilies as kin.
Shone like the sun 'til summer was done,
And saw a new season begin.

Fall she did as the equinox bid,
And her leaves came tumbling down.
From green to gold and other so bold,
Made a carpet weaved to astound.

In winter repose in the deepest of snows,
She slept in the darkest of nights.
Wooly and warm heard the alarm,
And awoke with the perception of light.

Round and round the seasons go round,
A top spinning off into space.
Silent in part tho' trilled like a lark,
A time clock with hands on its face.

April 2023

NOTHING IN COMMON

Let's recall our halcyon days,
The good ol' days of yore.
When I forsook other toys,
And coveted the shore.

While the sun beat down, I swam around,
Beginning to hit my stride.
When lo and behold I stubbed my toe,
Slighting a Big White's pride.

His eyes were matte, like a bat,
Black as the ace of spades.
Held all the cards, spoke like the bard,
Wearing a pair of shades.

I didn't holler, thought him a scholar,
From the folds beneath his chin.
With bottle-thick glasses worn for his classes,
Saw a tenuous friendship begin.

From time to time, we'd revisit to find,
We didn't have much in common.
I had no teeth and he had no feet,
I was Catholic and he was Mormon.

Often had lunch, when I had a hunch,
It was time to part and scoot.
'Cause my friend said he just loved Italian,
And I a yen for shark fin soup.

April 2023

A PLEA

Reject us not for the things we've done,
Things that we regret.
Things that bade Your Son don flesh,
To satisfy our debt.

Restore the love lost afore,
Renewed upon a cross.
Heal our souls dimmed by sin,
Cleanse us from our dross.

Hear our hail 'n' holy praise,
We offer now each day.
To seek your pardon 'n' parole,
And mend our wounded ways.

Our faith once nil defied your will,
Until opened to The Word.
Who raised our minds to better things,
'Yond other things we'd heard.

Having lived too long in your disfavor,
We began once more to see.
To understand beyond mere sight,
What Christ's sacrifice asks we be.

Our prize could be endless days,
In glory sans an end.
In the presence of love itself,
A joy beyond our ken.

April 2023

BEAUTY FRAMED

The light is drawn before the dawn,
To see the sun arise.
In brilliant hues it bespeaks of you,
Who sets but never dies.

Brings to mind The Spirit nigh,
Who creates the things we see.
Things that were 'n' came to light,
And other things to be.

O beauty bright that casts her light,
In diverse and sundry ways.
Warms the heart that recalls in part,
First loves and former days.

Beauty framed is not the same,
As beauty dearly loved.
For which we cry and often die,
For the eternal love above.

Deep within where beauty lies,
Love may rise and shine.
But love at times may fall aside,
And die upon the vine.

While beauty framed may retain its fame,
And depend on museum walls.
Age suggests we turn the page,
And enjoy what we can recall.

April 2023

ETERNAL MIND

Long before storm and sea,
When time was yet to be.
Forever in the eternal mind,
Are thoughts of you and me.

Love that is but never was,
The Sprit of Three is He.
The creator of eternal life,
The seed to grow a tree.

Animates all who will ever be,
Regardless of the source.
The primary cause that shapes us all,
The everlasting force.

Asks us to return to dust,
When time has run its course.
Embraces all who heeds His call,
With joy and no remorse.

Worth more than we deserve,
Forever on His mind.
Showers us with gifts 'n' things,
To live our lives in kind.

Beyond the ken of feeble men,
He loves us to the end.
The reality He leaves to us,
Which never we contend.

March 2023

LOST & FOUND

King Tut saw the goddess Mut,
Walk across the sky.
Hoped one day he'd walk that way,
When he said his last goodbye.

Took a spin to his chagrin,
While charioting on the plain.
Hit a rut, the boy King Tut,
Flying into fame.

Wrapped him up with pitch 'n' stuff,
And placed him in a tomb,
With so many things for future use,
Barely had the room.

With treasures bright they shone at night,
With a radiant mask of gold.
A nest of sarcophagi to protect his Ka,
As The Book of the Dead foretold.

Lay safe and sound within the ground,
Untouched for many years.
Secure from robbers' picks,
Unlike his other peers.

Found at last to great renown,
Intact and undefiled.
Celebrated for his great escape,
The world is still beguiled.

There's a debate of late, it's another's tomb,
Repurposed for his use.
If so, imagine the wealth in other tombs,
That were defiled 'n' much abused.

March 2023

THE HAND

A tightly clenched hand, rose from the sand,
Desperate for exhumation.
A symbol of might that just came to light,
Seeking renewal and restoration.

Lost to time as Kemet declined,
Sought rescue and reanimation.
A granite colossus that emerged from the past,
To praise and exaltation.

Who might he be, this hand breaking free,
A stoic pharaonic creation.
Who stood at his post, fiercer than most,
Guarding glyphs from desecration.

Grim face 'n' all and twenty feet tall,
Drew raves from its very inception.
Was likely the guardians of sphinxes,
And the protector of priestly processions.

Be it intact or apart, a stone sculptor's art,
Was a gift from the sand for the ages.
Brought to sight by a sandstorm at night,
To the delight of Egyptian sages.

What else might there be, that we want to see,
Beneath the deserts of ancient Kemet.
Perhaps hidden away for some other day,
May be the incantations of the goddess Selket.

March 2023

VULCANOLOGY

Lava is disgorged from Vulcan's Forge,
Deep in the bowels of Etna.
Now half blind, wears a patch at times,
To protect a damaged retina.

Concocts a stew few can chew,
With igneous rocks and fire.
Labors in glee in the hope he'll see,
Destruction and folks expire.

For mischief's sake, bakes a lava cake,
As a dark 'n' unique deception.
Magma below then blows Earth's crust,
For shock and intimidation.

Bubblers, while dangerous, are still beautiful,
Creating streams of light at night.
But the big guys rise to the occasion,
And remove the sun from sight.

Ashes fall as high-risers stall,
Entombing the world in white.
Often suffocating an endangered populace,
Who huddle and cower in fright.

Pyroclastic flows now enter the show,
And level everything in sight.
The most vicious of nature's phenomena,
Are an awesome display of might.

Yet all's not grim when at the rim,
Of a silent and dormant crater.
'Cause they've made islands rise to great surprise,
From eruptions early on and later.

While volcanoes may appear inactive, tho,
Some lie surreptitiously in wait.
'Cause Vulcan still plots in Mt. Etna,
Considering future dates.

March 2023

IMAGINE

Imagine being naked,
Displayed upon a tree.
Embarrassed for heaven's sake,
And the likes of you 'n' me.

Flesh all torn, like clothes once worn,
Disguised his angst 'n' fears.
For the purpose He was born,
A baptism of tears.

Imagine, too, the deed agreed,
Between Father and The Son.
The Spirit's role in the great amen,
That The Father's will be done.

Tho' he'd don the flesh a woman made,
He was everybody's son.
Raised to die to sanctify,
The sacrifice of One.

As passions go, He was the first to know,
That redemption was now at hand.
Dread the thought that He'd be dead,
But He was God as well as man.

Came alive to satisfy,
The debt He had to pay.
Due a merciful 'n' loving Father,
Disobeyed by those dismayed.

Imagine, too, how great the love,
To forgive those who cause such pain.
Raise them up on the final day,
And be reconciled again.

Imagine!

March 2023

FULL CIRCLE

Round and round forever after,
Without a beginning or end.
An eternal presence ever glorious,
Upon whom we all depend.

The Godhead exists in perpetuity,
Without a future or a past.
A present beyond our prescience,
A concept too difficult to grasp.

Seemingly remote but ever near,
We're reminded of His eternal presence.
Found in the beauty of Mother Nature,
Which attests to His ultimate essence.

Love and beauty hand in hand,
An evergreen and perennial union.
Flowing from His mind to enlighten mankind,
With the hope of eternal communion.

Wreathes symbolize the everlasting journey,
When we celebrate the Christmas story.
Tho' born to the flesh, He created the world,
Coming full circle in majesty and glory.

November 2022

WINGS

Wings of a butterfly, wings of a bee,
Wings of gulls surveying the sea.
Hummingbird wings so fast nobody sees,
Wings on His angels, God so decrees.

Birds of a feather made to be one,
Kindred spirits that fly to the sun.
Flittering and fluttering, rise in the air,
Never alit in fear or despair.

Creatures of nature made free of care,
Beheld in their beauty ever so rare.
Breasted and crested in colors they soar,
Some to great heights, some found indoors.

Wings of an eagle, wings of a hawk,
Birds of prey at which people gawk.
With beaks 'n' talons sharp for a kill,
Circle in wait espying each rill.

Some rise on thermals with nary a flap,
Migrate to places all over the map.
Seeing them leave causes no tears,
For we know they'll return as they do every year.

Winged creatures bear sundry names,
Some hunted for the table 'n' considered fair game.
It would be a great loss 'n' much to our shame,
If they didn't come back 'n' we were to blame.

October 2022

THE LAST RESORT

Montauk makes a valid point,
As boats come into port.
Perceived to be the end of land,
It's now the last resort.

Its symbol is tall and stately,
Clad in red and white.
An old and historic lighthouse,
Warning of perils unseen at night.

Rotates its head so beams be shed,
To mariners far at sea.
Alerting ships to hidden shoals,
When listing far to lee.

Considered passé to the new today,
No longer plies its trade.
Now a museum to display the wares,
Artisans deftly made.

Montauk forever makes the point,
If its happiness you seek.
Montauk is the beginning not the end,
Unless you're going further East.

September 2022

THE BEACH

Come away to the beach one day,
When the flags are running green.
See summer at its very best,
Amid the yells and screams.

See the waves assail the shore,
The adventurous roiled in sand.
Tossing the brave round 'n' round,
Finding it hard to stand.

Some ride the crests with great finesse,
Sliding smoothly to the shore.
Shaking their hair of the sand ensnared,
Carefree amid the roar.

Exhausted they flop on a blanket there,
Basking a while in the sun.
Then turn over to the obverse side,
Sensing the back is done.

Umbrellas in myriad colors,
Flutter and flap in the breeze.
Proliferate across the seascape,
To afford the fair reprieve.

The gulls swooping 'n' soaring,
Seeking a morsel to eat.
Snatching a fry before somebody's eyes,
Cawing for another treat.

All is oblivious to the eyes of lovers,
Who meander across the strand.
With only eyes for each other,
Preoccupied hand in hand.

August 2023

FULL OF GRACE

Stars in the highest heaven,
Await the maiden full of grace.
The Immaculata foretold in scripture,
The pride of the human race.

Stars vie for a place in her circlet,
A crown for Heaven's queen.
That graces her head 'n' countenance,
Sets her apart from others seen.

The ark of the incarnation,
Virgin Mother of God's only son.
Her "yes" resounds through the ages,
So again God 'n' man be one.

Devoted to the needs of family,
Endured a hegira to Egypt in strife.
Bore the loss of her dear companion,
But thankful for being his wife.

Suffered the pangs of her Son's passion,
Witnessed His victory 'n' glorious rise.
Counseled His church and apostles,
'Til the time of her brief demise.

The entire firmament pays her homage,
Stars reflect the light of her face.
Recognizing twelve stars insufficient,
To hail Mary full of grace.

July 2022

GOOD JUDGEMENT

After the Final Judgement,
All things will be created anew,
Old wineskins will be forgotten,
And the sky a deeper blue.

Bodies and souls will be reunited,
In a profound 'n' glorified way.
Transfigured like their savior,
Like sunshine on summer's day.

Choice meals will be served at His table,
With plenty to drink and eat.
Suggesting body functions will continue,
Mansions promised ours to keep.

Will all our questions be answered,
Will we be equal or loved by degree.
Will we still be free to choose?
Meet all we wanted to see.

Will the joy we'll feel in His presence,
The beauty of The Holy Place.
Satisfy every curiosity 'n' desire,
As the ultimate blessing 'n' grace?

Will we understand the Beatific Vision,
The role of the spirit in three.
Know those who lost God's love forever,
Get to know what I was meant to be.

Assuming the scales weigh in my favor,
Understanding there's no guarantee.
I look forward to love God forever,
The destiny He wanted for me.

May 2022

BEDTIME

I hate to go to bed at night,
I find no rest or peace.
My mind remains on overdrive,
Thoughts just never cease.

If I'm not searching for a coda,
It's the beginning of a plea,
Petitions never seem to work,
'Cause my mind won't let me be.

Up and down the years go round,
Revisiting with he and she.
Back to places I've previously been,
And places I'd like to see.

On the Grand Tour that the elite endure,
On a cruise without a pause.
Or the hero in an unstaged play,
Sans the crowd's applause.

I twist and turn and hope to learn,
The night is almost done.
Only to discover it's just started,
And it's only a quarter to one.

It would be unfair to put things to rest,
When the writer cannot sleep.
For the quandary of an inquisitive mind,
Just too active 'n' much too deep.

April 2023

OLD GLORY

Danger bids the flag unfurl,
And her sons and daughters rise.
To protect the weak 'n' vanquish the foe,
Today and times gone by.

Citizen warriors who answer the call,
When a wounded nation cries.
Put lives at risk in perilous times,
To forestall that tyranny abide.

Forever loved but desecrated in ignorance,
The mercurial too belie.
The values Old Glory holds dear,
For which many bravely fought 'n' died.

A blue field of stars with red 'n' white bars,
The banner revered 'n' held high.
Dishonored by those who distort our rights,
Secured under the flag they decry.

Long may it wave o'er the home of the brave,
In recollection of heroes that die.
By a legion who celebrates fallen brothers 'n' sisters,
And keeps memories forever alive.

Allegiance is pledged to blood that was shed,
To preserve the land we adore.
The flag we salute on march 'n' parade,
Since the colonies were twelve 'n' one more.

April 2022

BELIEVE

Where am I going?
Where have I been?
Somewhere 'tween goodness,
And the darkness of sin.

White as a lily,
Black as a crow.
Gray as a footprint,
Aging in snow.

Journey to somewhere,
Where I don't know.
Arrive when I get there,
Just have to go.

I look for a place,
That beckons to me.
Where joy is eternal,
And where I long to be.

It's on a high mountain,
The gate that I seek.
Guarded by angels,
At the top of its peak.

Pray they embrace me,
And usher me in.
To a place of true beauty,
Where the elect dwell within.

So brilliant its glory,
The sun ebbs in its light.

Where time has expired,
And there's no day and no night.

Radiant are all faces,
Colors glow too.
Red as Christ's wounds,
And Our Lady true blue.

Crystal clear to my vision,
Is what I wish to see.
The reality of The Trinity,
That great mystery.

The light shines the brightest,
Where God sits enthroned.
The center of all wisdom,
And The Credo's entoned.

Like a gazelle aleaping,
I'll bound o'er the hills.
Partake of choice fare,
Whenever God wills.

Thank the saints whose prayers,
Intercede for all men.
On whom, with our loved ones,
Our ascension depends.

The love will be endless,
That much I know.
But that's about all,
We can imagine below.

What God's prepared for the holy,
Can't possibly be conceived.
And what's in store for the elect,
No one would believe.

January 2022

THE WOOD

Glory, glory here's a story,
A Babe born to the wood.
Sweet and gentle, mild 'n' holy,
Love's epitome 'n' jolly good.

Long awaited ever fated,
To stand where Adam stood.
Born anew to mend the broken,
As God in mercy thought He should.

Where the dew fell, grew a sapling,
In a glade as green as jade.
Delighted those of faith before Him,
To fulfill the promises God has made.

Ever graceful 'n' always fruitful,
Bore ripe and Luscious fruit.
In an orchard in need of pruning,
Came The Word to proclaim the truth.

A sacrifice then a triumph,
Once subject to flail and nail.
On a fallen tree depended,
A wooden witness to be hailed.

Crossed her arms to bear His body,
Sap ran red to feel His pain.
Rose again to seed the garden,
To become a symbol of His reign.

December 2021

ONE WORD

So much has been spoken,
    So many things said.
So much has been written,
    So many things read.

Of the words ever uttered,
    Only one Word avails.
The author of creation,
    Whose utility prevails.

The Word made the universe,
    In the blink of an eye.
Turned on the lights,
    With stars in the sky.

Brought continents into being,
    With oceans aside.
East and west rivers,
    That mountains divide.

Begot man in His image,
    With a mate by his side.
Tempered justice with love,
    When tempted by pride.

Silent in creation,
    But still understood.
Nary a word spoken,
Tho' saying: "It was good!"

December 2021

MIRROR IMAGES

Saw a boy in the rear-view mirror,
Sadly left behind.
Sped off on a four-lane highway,
With other things in mind.

Avoided the straight and narrow,
For fear of laws enforced.
The detours that stifle progress,
Citations at a cost.

Basked in the illusion of freedom,
Enticed by sheen and gloss.
Thought happiness was on the freeway,
But found that way led to loss.

The narrow road for its challenges,
The occasional pits and flaws.
Is the only way to paradise,
As holy people know.

Fortunately, saw an off-ramp,
With directions from above.
Pointing the way to heaven,
For joy and eternal love.

Again saw the youth in the mirror,
A wiser version of me.
Walking the straight and narrow,
Enroute to joy and thee.

November 2021

THE GIFT

If St. Nicholas was a shepherd,
On that cold 'n' star-lit night.
He'd rejoice at the lamb he found,
Swaddled all in white.

Would be in awe at the scene he saw,
A family haloed bright.
A newborn Babe on a bed of straw,
The holiest of sights.

Like Christmas cards sent each year,
To celebrate His birth.
In holy repose or winter snows,
For children's glee 'n' mirth.

He put aside his bag of coins,
Firs and wreaths of green.
Pale against three wisemen's gifts,
Their measure of esteem.

Out of place with a ruddy face,
Clad in red and white.
Gave up his crook for a story book,
Was gone at early light.

Left his flock for antler stock,
And returned to future climes.
Change His name to Santa Claus,
In keeping with the times.

Children He now delights,
With gifts from a sleigh in flight.
But he knows the greatest gift he ever saw,
Is the Babe he saw that night.

November 2021

MUST BE LOVE

He is much too far beyond me,
Tho' I feel Him very near.
Beyond my understanding,
Yet I know that He is here.

A mystery that reveals Himself,
In an unknown voice I hear.
A voice that often guides me,
Until the time I fear.

Not only close beside me,
I sense that He's within.
To animate the soul I have,
And have my life begin.

Known from the beginning,
So I have been told.
Though I hardly even know Him,
He's been my friend from old.

Never interferes with me,
No matter what I do.
Disregards the things I say,
Tho' my deeds maybe taboo.

He's given me a conscience,
Which I can nurture if I choose.
Even an angelic counselor,
If I wish to hear his views.

He's said to be forgiving,
When my ways have gone awry.
His mercy is unlimited,
Until the day I die.

Why does He even bother,
Why waste His precious time.
I'm unworthy of His attention,
Yet love makes Him so inclined.

If it isn't love that moves Him,
Eternal and Divine.
It's all we can surmise,
To understand this rhyme.

September 2021

BLESSED MOUNTAIN

Behold the holy mountain,
Awash in glory's light.
A beacon for the ages,
And pilgrims through the night.

Hoary white in rising,
Magnificent from afar.
Rises from the depths of creation,
Ancient like the stars.

It welcomes saints 'n' the holy,
The poor, weak and strong.
The rich who survived the camel's eye,
Who forsake ways gone wrong.

Found in the company of angels,
At the edge of the glassy sea,
Where crowns are cast in worship,
Of the One God made of three.

For those who meet the challenge,
Survive every crag and bog.
The reward is life eternal,
In the presence of Almighty God.

Behold the blessed mountain,
Holy sanctuary and more.
That bids souls come to paradise,
That men enjoyed before.

August 2021

FEET OF CLAY

I dip my quill in bitter gall,
To assess the fate of Rome.
The conqueror of so many lands,
It thought the world its own.

Sent legions to impose its will
On rival states 'n' fields.
Bearing eagles aloft on golden staffs,
And lightning bolts on shields.

Culture traveled within the van,
To justify Roman might.
Slavery grew as structures rose,
To great and awesome heights.

Temples mollified the conquered,
With a pantheon to adore.
Stadia to entertain thousands,
And basilicas for sundry stores.

Art and innovation introduced,
But at a price few could pay.
For freedom lost is a heavy cost,
Despite what Romans say.

Pristine togas belied the schemes,
That the pompous sometimes play.
And so Caesars fell to rival foes,
And Rome to feet of clay

August 2021

A PRIVILEGE

There is no greater privilege,
Than to serve Jesus Christ Our Lord.
Wear His bitter crown of thorns,
Spare Him scourge and sword.

Relieve Him of the tree he bore,
The leafless sin of Cain.
The wood that tore flesh from bone,
That caused Him grievous pain.

Trust a heart so full of love,
His mercy over-flows.
Wipe His face to find a trace,
And have His features show.

Bear His wounds 'n' share His plight,
Know His grace is near.
Unite with Him to save poor souls,
Remove their flaws and fear.

Return His love 'n' blessed gifts,
Bestowed without a cost.
Carry the cross without remorse,
Regain what once was lost.

Accept His invitation,
To the feast he holds on high.
Where choice meats 'n' wine are served,
And the privileged never die.

September 2021

GARDENS

The Son rises from the altar,
The sun from the wine-dark sea.
Creation reflects its author,
One of the Holy Three.

Raised by the saintly 'n' holy,
Nailed to branches of a tree.
Expressed as the Word by His Father,
Sacrificed to set men free.

A debt repaid by innocence,
A healer in need of balm.
A lamb that came to the slaughter,
Limp in His mother's arms.

Depended in bitter sorrow
Depressed by the weight of sin.
Angels kneel to adore Him,
So, the world be renewed again.

A story that began in a garden,
Groans heard at the foot of a tree.
A garden that entombed His body,
Then saw glory and majesty.

The Son arose from the garden,
The sun from the depths of the sea.
The Word the alpha 'n' omega,
Who reigns for eternity.

July 2021

THE SOWER

The seeds, the awns, the barley's own,
Wheat fields to and fro.
The stalks, the cobs, the ears of corn,
The rows of grain we sow.

How they grow God only knows,
His miraculous touch no doubt.
The soil is tilled to yield His boon,
To reap 'n' glean each sprout.

Made the clouds to weep on high,
Tears to make them thrive.
The dew that falls that bids they rise,
In the morn to stay alive.

Arrayed in bloom like the harvest moon,
In tune with the farmer's sigh.
Each plant grows to appropriate size,
From Rhizomes to ever high.

Much we owe to the sun to rise,
The star of heat and light.
Whose rays are splayed in marvelous ways,
To foster nature's birth.

Yet had the sower not sown the seed,
On the Earth's first turn and morn.
The land would still be poorly worn,
For nothings would have grown.

June 2021

NO OTHER

How can there be one greater than He,
Who lights the stars at night.
Dims the moon before every noon,
And is righteous in all His might.

Created things like Saturn's rings,
To heaven's joy and delight.
Has the skies roil to moisten the soil,
And the sun to bathe us in light.

Created us out of primordial dust,
In an image that He designed.
An infinite being of body 'n' soul,
Destined for heavenly climes.

How can there be another like He,
Worthy of glory and praise,
Created the angels 'n' men like me,
With the promise of endless days.

He's ever, never, 'n' forever and more,
A circle who's never squared.
A God of three, One tho' He be,
A divinity with two others paired.

Make what we will from man's paper-mill,
Faux gods evil and vain.
None will survive other than He,
No matter their frivolous claims.

May 2021

ABOUT THE AUTHOR

Michael P. Mallardi was born in East Harlem, on St. Patrick's Day, March 17, 1934. Raised in Flushing, N.Y., Michael received a scholarship to a Catholic military academy, where he graduated as valedictorian of his class. He then matriculated at the University of Notre Dame where he received a degree in philosophy, magna cum laude.

Michael joined the American Broadcasting Company in 1956. He left for positions at MGM, Radio Press International, and as Vice President and General Manager of The Straus Broadcasting Group, then returned to ABC as Vice President of Corporate Planning. Thereafter, he became President of ABC Record and Tape Sales Corp. and then, ABC's Chief Financial Officer. He also became one of three of ABC's Executive Vice Presidents and was elected to its Board of Directors in October 1976.

Upon sale of ABC to Capital Cities, Inc. in 1986, Michael was appointed Senior Vice President and President of the Capital Cities/ABC Broadcast Group, the only senior corporate officer retained by the acquiring company. As such, he was responsible for the network-owned TV stations, all radio operations, and, for several years, its Video Enterprise activities and interests in ESPN, A&E, and Lifetime. He was also responsible for the network's broadcast operations and engineering activities, during a transition period for Capital Cities senior executives. Michael retired from ABC in 1996.

Michael was a founding trustee of the J.P. Morgan Mutual Funds and was on the board of the EEX Corporation, an oil exploration company in Houston, Texas. He also served as pro bono chairman of the Bon Secours Health System. In addition, he served on the boards of the American Women's Development Corporation (AWED), the Committee for Economic Development, Jr. Achievement of N.Y.,

International Radio and Television Society and Maximum Service Television (MSTV).

Michael and Sylvia, his wife of 63 years, have two daughters, Karen and Stephanie, and a loving granddaughter, Natalie Joan, who has been Michael's sunshine from the moment of her birth.

Parenthetically, Michael's older brother, Joseph, was the CEO of a French-owned company and a recipient of France's Legion of Honor.

www.ingramcontent.com/pod-product-compliance
Lightning Source LLC
Chambersburg PA
CBHW071756120626
46550CB00002B/816